ALTERNATOR
BOOKS™

ROBOT COMPETITIONS

MARY LINDEEN

D1412559

Lerner Publications ◆ Minneapolis

For Benjamin, champion of technology

Lerner Publications Company
A division of Lerner Publishing Group, Inc.
241 First Avenue North
Minneapolis, MN 55401 USA

For reading levels and more information, look up this title at www.lernerbooks.com.

Library of Congress Cataloging-in-Publication Data

Names: Lindeen, Mary, author.
Title: Robot competitions / Mary Lindeen.
Description: Minneapolis : Lerner Publications, [2017] | Series: Cutting-edge robotics | Audience: Ages 8–12. | Audience: Grades 4 to 6. | Includes bibliographical references and index.
Identifiers: LCCN 2016044531 (print) | LCCN 2016048575 (ebook) | ISBN 9781512440102 (lb : alk. paper) | ISBN 9781512449365 (eb pdf)
Subjects: LCSH: Robots—Juvenile literature. | Robotics—Juvenile literature | Contests—Juvenile literature. | Educational technology—Juvenile literature.
Classification: LCC TJ211.2 .L55846 2017 (print) | LCC TJ211.2 (ebook) | DDC 629.8/92—dc23

LC record available at https://lccn.loc.gov/2016044531

Manufactured in the United States of America
1-42272-26129-1/24/2017

CONTENTS

SLOW SOCCER

A soccer player slowly takes tiny steps toward an orange ball and then gives the ball a soft kick. It slowly rolls toward the net. But the goalie hardly even reacts.

This might sound like a pretty boring soccer game. But what if you knew the players were actually **robots**, and this game was an international championship game? The RoboCup is a robot competition that invites scientists and inventors to experiment with new technologies in a fun way. Teams build and program robots to play against one another. Eventually, **roboticists** hope to build a team of robots that can compete against—and even beat—human World Cup champions. Those who compete at RoboCup share computer **software**, robot designs, and other good ideas with one another to help develop better robots. One day you just might see humans playing against robots!

A RoboCup soccer game takes place in China in 2015.

CHAPTER 1

BEGINNING BATTLES

Robots can do many amazing things. So it makes sense that the people who invent these amazing machines would want to compare their designs and find out which robot is the biggest, the fastest, the smartest, or the strongest. In the world of robot competitions, the challenge and creativity of robot building meets the excitement of sporting events. But robot competitions actually have their roots in a much quieter game.

Contestants work with their robots during a 2014 competition in China.

Programmers gather around Robert Q, a computer programmed to play chess. The computer was beaten in its first competition with a human in 1967.

CHESS CHALLENGE

In 1967 Richard Greenblatt finished writing a computer program called MacHack. This was the first computer program that let a computer play a game of chess against a human. This computer program became a model for other similar computer programs. These days, chess players often use computer programs to help them practice and get better at playing the game.

Like computers, robots are programmed to complete certain tasks. And in robotic competitions, robots use computer programs to compete in their events. The computer programs used in robotic competitions can trace their beginnings to the same kind of software programs that were used to run that first game of chess.

Computer programmer David Slate plays a game of chess using a computer in 1970.

A roboticist picks up his micromouse from a maze during the 2013 International Robot Exhibition in Tokyo, Japan.

FROM BATTLES TO BEAUTY

Computers can compete, but they cannot move. Robots *can* move, and some of the earliest robotic competitions challenged robots to move in new ways. The Amazing Micromouse Competition, held in New York in 1979, challenged small robotic mice to find their way out of a maze. In 1989 the Critter Crunch in Denver, Colorado, was the first competition in which robots tried to destroy one another.

After these first competitions, many more contests developed. There is a World Robot Olympiad, which is like a robot Olympics for students. Events include soccer games, bowling tournaments, and other challenges. RobotArt is a competition that combines technology and art. Teams compete to build robots that make beautiful artwork. Then the public votes for the art they like best. The technology of robots is always changing—and so are robotics competitions!

Robots made by students play a soccer game during the World Robot Olympiad in 2016.

FACTOID!

Robotics competitions are like athletic competitions in many ways. Both have teams, coaches, winners, and rules. In fact, some schools consider robotics competitions an official sport. In 2012 Minnesota was the first state to make robotics competitions an official school sport for all of its schools.

Students cheer on Lego robots during a 2013 Robot Expo.

CHAPTER 2

CHECKING OUT THE COMPETITION

Not every robot competition is meant for every robot. Each contest has its own rules and challenges. Some competitions are for kids only. Other competitions are open to people of all ages. Competitions can be small local contests or huge international competitions. Every contest is different. But all of them give roboticists opportunities to create, compete, and come up with important ideas about how robots can be used in the real world.

Students watch as their robots complete an obstacle course.

FACTOID!

One popular competition is called FIRST (For Inspiration and Recognition of Science and Technology) Lego League. Students are given a challenge and then form teams to brainstorm solutions to real-world issues and build a Lego robot to perform a series of tasks. The challenge changes every year, but it may have to do with anything from garbage to natural disasters.

LET THE GAMES BEGIN!

Some robot contests showcase exciting challenges. In combat contests, robots fight against one another. Sumo robots try to push each other out of a ring, just like human sumo wrestlers do. Other robots compete in soccer and hockey, or they race against one another or lift weights. Robots even play laser tag in some contests!

FACTOID!

The UAV Challenge is one of the largest robotics contests in the world. It is held in Australia every year. In one challenge, known as the Outback Rescue, teams build unmanned **aerial** vehicles (UAVs), or **drones**, that can help with search-and-rescue missions. In the contest, robots find and rescue a life-sized **mannequin** named Outback Joe.

Drones similar to this one may be used in search-and-rescue missions.

Other contests require robots to complete some kind of task. They might have to find their way through a maze. Or a robot might have to be able to do something humans do, such as walk across a slippery floor or rough gravel without falling down. Contests for drones might require robots to fly through an aerial obstacle course. Other drone contests might test speed. There are even contests for underwater robots that are held in swimming pools!

Students prepare for a RoboRugby competition in Dublin, Ireland.

AND THE WINNER IS . . .

Another cool feature of robot competitions is the prizes. Roboticists work hard, and they deserve recognition for the important work they do. As in other contests, winners of robotics competitions often get medals, ribbons, or trophies. Winners might also get a free trip to compete in the next round of a contest. Or they might win an educational **scholarship**. Some contests even award cash prizes to the winners. In some competitions, you can win $1 million—or more!

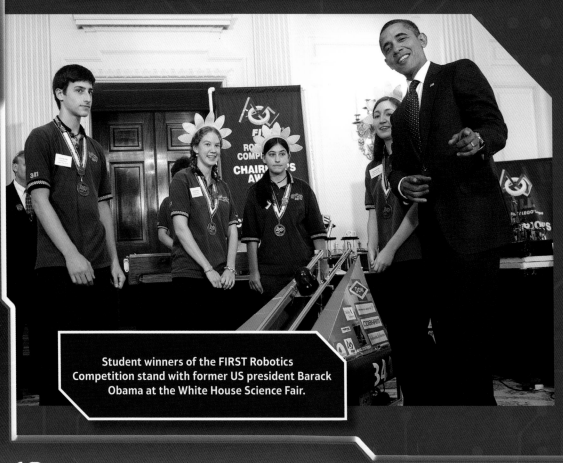

Student winners of the FIRST Robotics Competition stand with former US president Barack Obama at the White House Science Fair.

FACTOID!

Along with robots, many robotics competitions require reports, presentations, and even advertising to gain support for the team and the competition. Having good writing, speaking, and business skills is helpful in a robot competition. You'll also need good problem-solving, logic, and teamwork skills, as well as lots of creative thinking.

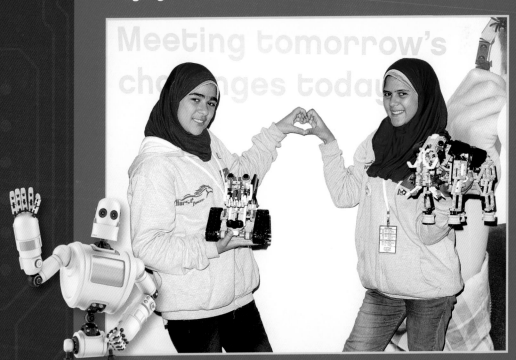

Students pose with their robots at a Lego Education FIRST Robot Games Tournament.

CHAPTER 3

THE SCIENCE BEHIND ROBOT COMPETITIONS

All robotics competitions require participants to know how to design, build, program, operate, and test robots. Robotics involves knowledge of science, technology, engineering, and math, or STEM—and every part of STEM has many more parts, from biology to computer science. This means roboticists have to have a lot of knowledge that's based in many different scientific fields. Then they have to put all of that STEM learning together to make a robot.

Students work to program their robot.

Engineers pose with robot hands called SoftHands. These hands have similar features to human hands.

ROBOT BIOLOGY

It might seem as if programming or electricity is the most important thing to know for a robot competition. But biology, the science of plants and animals, is also very important. Roboticists want their robots to move just as a real human or animal does. Many competitions require robots to walk like humans. Other contests include challenges for robots that can crawl like a bug or slither like a snake. So roboticists study biology to figure out how to make their robot as realistic as possible.

FACTOID!

Most robots are built out of hard materials that don't change shape. Soft robotics is a new field that involves building robots using materials that are soft and flexible. Soft robots can hold fragile objects and work more precisely than a typical robot. Contests to develop soft robotics are one of the newest additions to the world of robot competitions.

A new robotic arm demonstrates its ability to hold small, fragile objects at an event in Germany.

A PROBLEM-SOLVING ROBOT

Another important part of both science and robot competitions is problem-solving. Those who study science, technology, and robotics are looking for answers to questions and solutions to problems. Robots can do a lot of work that humans cannot do. For example, robots can go in dangerous or very small places to detect and record information. Robot competitions encourage roboticists to think of new ways to solve problems. They may even have to solve problems in the middle of a competition if their robot stops working properly. Winning robot designs can lead to new technology that helps scientists solve real-world problems.

Students make repairs to their team's robot before showing it in a demonstration.

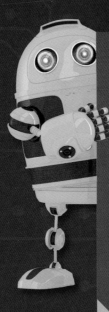

BOT THOUGHTS

Students who participate in robotics competitions are the scientists and inventors of the future. They learn how to do research and build **prototypes**. They learn to think through problems and work with a team to create solutions. They learn to be resourceful and persistent. And they learn that robotics can be challenging and exciting! Kids who participate in robotics competitions often go on to work in science, technology, engineering, and math, giving them the opportunity to make important changes in the world using their STEM skills.

CONTROLLING A ROBOT

Of course, a good robot also requires software systems that control how robots move and act. Software needs to be **coded** and programmed. A robot is also controlled using voice commands, computers, or remote controls, so roboticists need to know how electricity and signals work. They need to make sure their robots have the right **sensors** to be able to avoid obstacles or recognize a soccer ball and a goalpost. Robots also need to be able to follow commands from the roboticist or controller.

FACTOID!

Some competitions may require specialized knowledge. Along with general robotics skills, contestants in the NASA Student Rocket Launch Robotics Challenge have to know about space exploration and astronomy. The Marine Advanced Technology Education Underwater Robotics Competition requires an understanding of marine biology and oceanography. No matter what your interests are, there's probably a robotics competition that's perfect for you.

A roboticist works on her robot for a 2016 NASA robotics competition.

CHAPTER 4

THE FUTURE OF ROBOT COMPETITIONS

Technology is changing the field of robotics all the time. Computers become more powerful and much smaller. Scientists invent new materials to use for building robots. Smartphones and other communication tools make it possible for more people to share ideas. These changes are making it easier for more and more people around the world to experiment with robotics and enter competitions.

A robot developed to investigate a nuclear plant

New technology also makes it possible to build new kinds of robots. Waterproof materials led to underwater robotics competitions. Flying robots led to drone competitions. Microscopic computer parts led to **nanobot** competitions. Someday you might compete in a robot competition that's held at the North Pole, in outer space, or on the head of a pin!

Scientists created a life-sized cockroach robot, which could be used for spy missions.

BOT THOUGHTS

Robot competitions are fun. They are also useful. Scientists watch robot competitions to see what works and what doesn't. Inventors get new ideas from the successes and failures of robots in contests. Contest winners also often get attention from journalists and scientists around the world. This attention encourages schools, businesses, and government agencies to pursue more research in robotics. And more robotics research leads to more cool and helpful robots in the future.

In the future, more and more robots will be helping us at home, at school, and at work. Exactly what will those robots of tomorrow be doing? No one knows for sure. But you can get a sneak peek by checking out robot competitions. That's where some of the world's most creative robot enthusiasts come up with some of the best new ideas in robotics. Robot competitions show us the future!

Roboticists participate in a robot fighting contest in Tokyo, Japan, in 2002.

BOT PROJECT

You can use a toothbrush to make a small battery-powered robot that moves by vibrating. Race yours with a friend or set up an obstacle course for your vibrobot to get through. Experiment with different kinds of toothbrush heads to see which works best. You might decide to create an entire team of vibrobots and have your own Vibrobot Games.

WHAT YOU NEED

- 1 toothbrush with angled bristles (bristles must be all the same length)
- wire cutters or pliers
- 1 small vibrating motor (1 to 3 volts) from a pager, cell phone, or electric toothbrush
- 1 coin cell battery (1 to 3 volts)
- tape, rubber bands, foam tape, or zip ties

WHAT YOU DO

1. Ask an adult to help you with this project. Hold the head of the toothbrush. Cut the handle off the toothbrush. Be sure to leave about a half inch (1.3 centimeters) of the handle sticking out next to the bristles.

2. Strip the ends of the two wires on the motor. Put one wire on the top of the battery. Put the other wire on the bottom of the battery. The motor should spin or move in some way. (If it doesn't, you might have a bad battery or a bad motor or both.)

3. Use tape, a rubber band, foam tape, or a zip tie to secure the motor to the top of the toothbrush head along the handle stem.

4. Tape one of the motor wires to the bottom of the battery.

5. Use tape, a rubber band, foam tape, or a zip tie to secure the battery to the top of the toothbrush head. Make sure the wire on the bottom of the battery is between the toothbrush and the battery.

6. Attach the second wire to the top of the battery using tape, a rubber band, or a zip tie. The motor should be running. Your vibrobot should be jiggling and jumping and moving forward. Help a friend make one and have a race! Or compete with yourself: try modifying your vibrobot to see if you can get it to move faster, slower, or in a different direction. Happy hopping!

TIMELINE

1967 Richard Greenblatt writes MacHack, a computer program that plays chess against a human opponent.

1979 Small robotic mice compete to find their way out of a maze at the Amazing Micromouse Competition, held in New York City.

1989 The first robot battle competition, Critter Crunch, is held in Denver, Colorado.

1991 Flying robots compete in the first International Aerial Robotics Competition at the Georgia Institute of Technology.

1992 The first FIRST Robotics competition for high school students is held in New Hampshire.

1994 The first Robot Wars competition, which will become a popular TV show in England, is held in San Francisco.

1997 Nagoya, Japan, hosts the first RoboCup soccer tournament, which allows amateurs and professionals to compete with one another.

2002 The first Robo-One competition, which features humanoid robots, is held in Japan.

2016 The first international RobotArt competition is held, inviting students to create beautiful artwork using robots.

GLOSSARY

aerial: happening in the air

coded: given a set of instructions in a special computer language

drones: flying robots without a pilot that are operated by remote control

mannequin: a life-sized model of a human body

nanobot: a microscopic robot

prototypes: original models of something from which other forms are developed

roboticists: specialists who design, build, program, and experiment with robots

robots: machines that are programmed by a computer to do jobs that are usually performed by a person

scholarship: an amount of money given to a student to help pay for the student's education

sensors: instruments that can detect changes in heat, sound, pressure, and more and send that information to a controlling device

software: computer programs that control the workings of the equipment and direct it to do specific tasks

FURTHER INFORMATION

BattleBots
http://battlebots.com/videos

FIRST Robotics Competition
http://www.firstinspires.org/robotics/frc

Gilby, Nancy Benovich. *FIRST Robotics*. Ann Arbor, MI: Cherry Lake, 2016.

Lego: Cup Drop
http://www.lego.com/en-us/mindstorms/videos/gripp3r-in-cup-drop
-game-8216829ab570449ea2a4c112f5cffdd6

PBS Kids: Robot War
http://pbskids.org/dragonflytv/show/robotwar.html

Swanson, Jennifer. *National Geographic Kids Everything Robotics: All the Photos, Facts, and Fun to Make You Race for Robots*. Washington, DC: National Geographic Kids, 2016.

Ventura, Marne. *Google Glass and Robotics Innovator Sebastian Thrun*. Minneapolis: Lerner Publications, 2014.

INDEX

PHOTO ACKNOWLEDGMENTS

The images in this book are used with the permission of: background: © iStockphoto.
com/chekat; design elements: © iStockphoto.com/Kirillm; © iStockphoto.com/Ensup;
© 3alexd/iStock/Thinkstock; © iStockphoto.com/Ociacia; © kirill_makarov/Shutterstock.
com; © iStockphoto.com/Leo Blanchette; content: Shen Xiang/FEATURECHINA/Newscom,
p. 5; Guo Chen Xhinhua News Agency/Newscom, p. 6; AP Photo, p. 7; AP Photo/Edward
Kitch, p. 8; © EPA/Franck Robichon/Alamy, p. 9; Subhankar Chakraborty/Hindustan Times/
Newscom, p. 10; © Gary Friedman/Los Angeles Times/Getty Images, p. 11; AP Photo/the
Hearld-Palladium/Don Campbell, p. 12; © Lonny Garris/Shutterstock.com, p. 14; AP Photo/
Press Association , p. 15; © Jim Watson/AFP/Getty Images, p. 16; © Brendon Thorne/
Getty Images, p. 17; AP Photo/The Star, Brittany Randolph, p. 18; AP Photo/Georg Wendt/
picture-alliance/dpa, p. 19; © Martin Leiss/Bloomberg/Getty Images, p. 20; AP Photo/Doug
Strickland/Chattanooga Times Free Press, p. 21; NASA, p. 23; © Kiyoshi Ota/Bloomberg/
Getty Images, p. 24; Europics/Newscom, p. 25; © Kurita Kaku/Gamma-Rapho/Getty Images,
pp. 26-27; Larry Fisher/Quad-City Times/Newscom, p. 29.

Cover: © VCG/Getty Images (main); design elements: © iStockphoto.com/Kirillm;
© iStockphoto.com/chekat; © iStockphoto.com/da-vooda; © iStockphoto.com/Ensup;
© iStockphoto.com/eduardrobert.